D1825658

About this book

Think of the American West and you probably think of bandits: Billy the Kid and Jesse James; or famous US Marshals like Wyatt Earp. But the history of the West goes back further than that. It was 1804 when the first expedition set out to journey westward. Led by guides dressed in buckskins and raccoon-skin hats, the pioneers made their way over the Great Plains and across the Rocky Mountains to the Pacific.

Then came the Gold Rush, and townships grew rapidly all over California. But life was always hard. The immigrants had to build their own homes; the Red Indians were always hostile and the only means of communication were the Pony Express and the Wells Fargo stage.

This book traces the history of those hardy emigrants; of the difficulties that they met on the way, and the new lives they forged. It tells of covered wagons and railways, Mormons and forty-niners, Little Big Horn and the Alamo.

Some of the words in this book may be new to you. You can look them up in the word list on page 94.

AN EYEWITNESS HISTORY BOOK

Overland to the West

PAT HODGSON

Wayland

More Eyewitness History Books

The Railway Builders   Alistair Barrie
Pirates and Buccaneers   Tilla Brading
The Mayflower Pilgrims   Brenda Colloms
The Age of Drake   Leonard Cowie
Children of the Industrial Revolution   Penelope Davies
Country Life in the Middle Ages   Penelope Davies
Markets and Fairs   Jane Dorner
Newgate to Tyburn   Jane Dorner
Kitchens and Cooking   Kathy & Mike Eldon
The Story of the Cinema   Helen du Feu
The Story of the Wheel   Peter Hames
Men in the Air   Roger Hart
Popular Entertainment   Elizabeth Holt
A Victorian Sunday   Jill Hughes
Livingstone in Africa   Denis Judd
Stagecoach and Highwayman   Stephanie McKnight
The Tudor Family   Ann Mitchell
The Horseless Carriage   Lord Montagu
The Firefighters   Ann Mountfield
The Slave Trade   Ann Mountfield
Clothes in History   Angela Schofield
Florence Nightingale   Philippa Stewart
Sport through the Ages   Peter Wilson
The Glorious Age of Charles II   Helen Wodzicka
Ships and Seafarers   Helen Wodzicka
The Printer and his Craft   Helen Wodzicka
Road Transport   Susan Goldblatt
Shops and Shopping   Ann Mountfield
Shakespeare and his Theatre   Philippa Stewart
Tutankhamun's Egypt   Penelope Davies & Philippa Stewart
The Story of Medicine   Kathy & Mike Eldon
Toys in History   Angela Schofield
Tom-tom to Television   Kathy & Mike Eldon
Witchcraft and Magic   Pat Hodgson
Islam   Brenda Ralph Lewis
Animals in War   Pat Hodgson
Street Cries   Patricia Morrell
Steam Engines   Brenda Ralph Lewis
When Dinosaurs Ruled   Brenda Ralph Lewis
Greek Myth and Legend   Brenda Ralph Lewis
Beads, Barter and Bullion   Brenda Ralph Lewis

Frontispiece A fur trapper's cabin by Frederick Remington

ISBN 0 85340 439 9
Copyright © 1978 by Wayland Publishers Limited
First published in 1978 by Wayland Publishers Limited
49 Lansdowne Place, Hove, East Sussex.
BN3 1HF, England
Printed and bound in the UK by Morrison and Gibb Limited, Edinburgh

Contents

1. The Lonely Country

Everyone has a picture of life in an American frontier town from films, books and country-and-western songs. But Hollywood "westerns" usually just deal with the last thirty years of the nineteenth century. By this time pioneering was over, and the pattern of roads, railways and towns had been mapped out. This is the story of the first settlers in the West. People who trekked across the unknown land in search of a better life. In 1800 France, Spain and Mexico still held large areas of the American continent. The history of the West really begins with the Louisiana Purchase of 1803. In that year Thomas Jefferson (the President) bought from Napoleon a huge territory west of the Mississippi for fifteen million dollars.

The first explorers found a strange, lonely country, inhabited only by scattered Indian tribes. The pioneers were a mixed bunch of people. Some were natural loners, and liked to live on their wits in wild country. They often became fur trappers and traders. There was good money in this, and the phrase "make an easy buck" had its origin in the fur trade — trappers were paid a dollar for each buckskin. Missionaries also followed the trail west. But most of the would-be settlers were ordinary people, lured westward by the chance of better living conditions. They must have been adventurous and brave, because they had no promise of home, food or comfort at the end of their long and often terrible journey.

MERIWETHER LEWIS In 1804 Thomas Jefferson sent out an expedition to explore the territory recently bought from the French. It was led by Captain Meriwether Lewis and William Clark. Lewis posed for this portrait of himself in frontiersman's clothes shortly after his return. He is wearing a fringed buckskin over one shoulder, and a raccoon-skin hat. The explorers were away for over two years and their normal clothes would have worn out long before their journey was over. A hunting knife is at his belt, and he holds a long-barrelled rifle.

LEWIS AND CLARK MEET THE MANDAN INDIANS. Lewis and Clark spent their first winter with the Mandan Indians. Here they met a young Shoshone Indian called Sacagawea. He can be seen on the left of the picture. Sacagawea acted as guide and interpreter for the party when they went on in the spring. You can see the American explorers, still dressed in their city clothes, greeting the Indian chiefs outside their stockade. One of these chiefs worked out a route for the explorers to follow. On the right-hand side of the picture you can see a buffalo's head on a stick carried by one of the braves.

THE EXPLORERS BUILDING HUTS. In this picture
the explorers are busy building a log hut for the
winter. The drawing comes from a book written by
Patrick Gass about the Lewis and Clark expedition.
The artist did not actually go with the party, so he has
had to use his imagination. The upright poles look
rather unsteady and lop-sided, and it is unlikely that
the men would be wearing their top hats for the job.
The winter of 1804-5 was a very cold one. Lewis
recorded a temperature of forty-five degrees centi-
grade below zero one day.

EXPLORING THE MISSOURI RIVER. The expedition headed westward in the spring of 1805. The explorers followed the Missouri River until they came to its source in the Rocky Mountains. There were many mishaps on the journey, like the one shown in the picture. The artist has again made sure that the men have their top hats on. He also imagines that two horses could have got inside the canoe! Some parts of the Missouri were, in fact, very difficult to navigate, particularly the Great Falls. Here Lewis noted that the waterfall was 300 yards (about 300m) wide and at least 80 feet (24m) high.

THE FIRST HOSTILE INDIANS. Lewis and Clarke at last reached the Columbia River, which led down to the west coast of America and the Pacific Ocean. The return journey was easier, but there was one Skirmish with Blackfoot Indians, which is shown here. The Indians had tried to steal rifles and horses. One of them can be seen firing at Lewis. The explorer returned fire, and killed one of the Indians. According to Gass's book, Lewis could not have been wearing the frock coat he has on in the picture. He had bartered it for a canoe shortly before the shooting.

A MOUNTAIN MAN. In the early eighteenth century, the new unexplored territories of the West became the home of fur trappers and hunters. They were lonely pioneers known as "mountain men" because they set their beaver traps in the Rocky Mountains. This trapper wears a buckskin coat, leggings and a beaver-skin hat. He carries a heavy rifle, powerful enough to shoot buffalo or grizzly bear if necessary. He would also have several knives, and perhaps a pipe and tobacco. A spare horse carries his furs, and he would carry no food, preferring to live off the land.

THE ROCKY MOUNTAINS. These are the Rocky Mountains, the haunt of the mountain men. The mountains were lonely and beautiful, with dizzy heights and frightening abysses. There would usually only be animals for company. The covered wagon you can see on the road would not have attempted the journey until the 1840s. The Rockies were also known as the Shining Mountains. It was believed that they contained gold and silver, and precious stones.

TRAPPING A BEAVER. Here you can see a mountain man laying a beaver trap in a stream. Trappers would never shoot the animals as it would damage the fur. Instead they laid snares underwater. These would snap shut when touched, and trap the beaver until it was drowned. The traps were baited with green plants and lowered into the water on chains. In the top picture the hunter stands over one of his traps sharpening a stick to use for skinning his victim. He checks another trap in the bottom picture. Glimpses of the unfortunate beavers can be seen in the small round pictures.

A BEAVER HAT. Furs were very much in demand between 1810 and 1840 for hats and trimmings. Here is a fashionable man in a beaver hat. In New York a hat like this would have cost ten dollars. Women also had fur-trimmed dresses and bonnets. Beaver was the most popular but other furs like marten, fox and otter were also much prized. Unfortunately around 1840 fashions changed. The demand for beaver skins fell sharply as silk hats became popular. "Hell's full of high silk hats" the fur trappers grumbled.

BEARS. The mountain men saw many unfamiliar animals when they first journeyed in the lonely Rockies. Grizzly bears, which could weigh up to 450kg, would lurk in the forests. The explorers Lewis and Clark had some frightening experiences. Lewis recorded that he would rather ''fight two Indians than one bear''. Here one of the explorers has escaped up a tree. The artist has drawn a very strange-looking beast. This is because few people had seen a grizzly as they were only found in the West.

A TRAPPERS' CAMP. These fur trappers have chosen a sheltered spot in the forest for their camp. There are plenty of logs for the fire. The hunter in the middle is telling his friends how he shot the stag which is hanging from a branch on the right. The man in the foreground has a dog, which would be useful for fetching the birds shot for food. Some animal traps are lying on the ground. As hunters were on their own for most of the time, they enjoyed a meeting with friends round a warm camp fire.

FUR TRAPPERS AND THE INDIANS. This hunter has been frightened by hostile Indians while setting his traps in the river. Now he is going carefully into the forest to hide. The Blackfoot tribe hated the white men, particularly since Lewis had shot one of them. The trapper wears the usual buckskin clothes, with soft moccasins on his feet. His only hope is to hide. The Blackfoot would easily be able to capture him, in spite of his gun.

JIM BRIDGER. This photograph was taken in the 1860s. It shows Jim Bridger, one of the old mountain men. He first became a trapper in 1822 in answer to an advertisement in the *Missouri Gazette*. It asked for ''enterprising young men'' to work for the Rocky Mountain Trading Company. In later years he used to talk about his days as hunter and guide, saying: ''They said I was the damnedest liar that ever lived. That's what a man gets for telling the truth.''

21

KIT CARSON. Kit Carson was another famous mountain man. He had been a hunter since his teens. In the 1840s he joined John C Frémont's expedition to Oregon. Frémont wrote exciting stories about his travels. When ordinary American families heard the stories they also began to think of trying to take the Oregon Trail themselves. Later Carson became a brigadier general in the US Army, and a famous fighter of Indians. This photograph was taken in his army days. He still looks young, although he must have been in his middle fifties. He was the only US general who never learned to read or write.

FORT LARAMIE. Fort Laramie in east Wyoming was the home of the American Fur Company and one of the most important meeting places for the hunters. It was built by the Rocky Mountain Fur Company who called it Fort William. As you can see, it was built round a courtyard and had thick walls. There is a watchtower over the entrance, and there are similar towers on the three other outside walls. Trading is going on in the central courtyard where groups of Indians are talking with trappers.

THE ANNUAL MEETING. The high point of a trapper's year was the annual meeting or rendezvous between trappers, traders and Indians. Sometimes a hunter might have 300 to 400 skins to sell. At the rendezvous these were exchanged or bartered for food, new clothes, gunpowder, whisky and tobacco. Good prices were paid for pelts (fur skins), but the trappers usually drank or gambled the money away for one glorious month at the rendezvous. It was the traders who made the profit. As you can see, the annual encampment covered a large area. Some traders are riding into the general confusion of the camp. A hunter is playing cards with some Indians on the left hand side of the picture.

CATLIN'S PORTRAIT OF MAH-TO-TOH-PA. George Catlin journeyed westward in the early nineteenth century for a different reason from most men. He spent ten years living among the Indians, painting their portraits and writing about their customs. This is his portrait of a Mandan chieftain Mah-to-toh-pa.

In English, this means "the four bears". His robe is made out of two skins from mountain sheep. It is decorated with locks of human hair taken from the scalps of his enemies. He wears deerskin leggings and buckskin moccasins, embroidered with porcupine quills. Buffalo horns decorate his helmet.

HUNTING BUFFALO. When Catlin was living with the Mandan Indians there were still plenty of buffalo about. Catlin said that buffalo flesh tasted like fat beef and was delicious. The skin, horns, hooves and bones

were used to make clothes, shields and bows. The Indians rode fearlessly into the herds and shot the animals with bows and arrows. Catlin often rode beside the hunters to see exactly what was happening.

THE BUFFALO DANCE. The Mandan Indians needed a regular supply of buffalo. For this reason they sometimes performed this magical dance to bring the roaming animals back to the area. Catlin described how every brave had to own a buffalo mask. You can see that a strip of hair was left at the back of the mask which reached to the floor. The dancers have bows and arrows and knives and pretend to kill the mock buffalo. Catlin said that the dance never failed as the buffalo were usually not far away. Catlin was one of the last white men to see the Mandan Indians in their full glory. As the settlers arrived in the West they over-hunted the buffalo so that the herds gradually vanished. With the buffalo went the Indians' source of food. The Mandan tribe was almost completely wiped out in 1837 by smallpox, which they caught from white settlers.

2. The Long Trek

Following the trappers and hunters came the first true settlers to the West. These were the pioneer families who built houses and farmed the land. Some settlers could not resist the constant lure of unknown country and they often sold up their land and moved on after a few years. They risked the journey westward because they were poor and landless. This man is so poor that he can carry all he has in a couple of small bundles. His way west would first take him to St Louis. St Louis had grown up into a flourishing town because of the fur trade. There he might join up with a party journeying west by one of the recognized trails. It was always safer to travel in a group, and by the 1840s, plenty of guidance on equipment needed and the hazards of the route could be found in John Frémont's reports.

The Sante Fé Trail was the earliest way to the West. It led to the lands of the south-west, originally in Mexican hands, and was used by traders. The Oregon Trail closely followed the explorers' and fur trappers' route. Starting at Independence, Missouri, it crossed the Plains to the Rockies. From there it passed through a difficult area to the Columbia River and the Pacific. The California Trail followed the Oregon route as far as Fort Hall, Idaho, and then branched west. The first wave of exploration early in the century had been stimulated by the Louisiana Purchase of land from the French (see page 7). The second wave of colonization started in the 1840s when the United States gained Texas, California and New Mexico from the Mexicans. From this time the wagon trails of emigrant families really got going.

THE ALAMO. Some ranchers and hunters had gone into Texas while it was still part of Mexico. The Mexicans did not want them. In 1835 fighting broke out. The Mexicans trapped and slaughtered 180 Americans in the Alamo fort at San Antonio. The fort had been adapted from an old Spanish missionary station. You can see the church on the right. Mexican soldiers are climbing the walls which had once surrounded a monastery. The Americans defeated the Mexicans a few weeks later at the battle of San Jacinto, shouting as they attacked: "Remember the Alamo".

DAVY CROCKETT. A famous man in the history of the American West died at the Alamo. His name was Davy Crockett. His exploits were recorded in *Davy Crockett's Almanac* and made him a legend during his own lifetime. In the early days he was a bear hunter. In this picture he is wearing the fringed, buckskin jacket of the backwoodsman. A powder horn and beaverskin pouch are slung round his neck. It is said that Crockett killed fifteen of the enemy before he died at the Alamo.

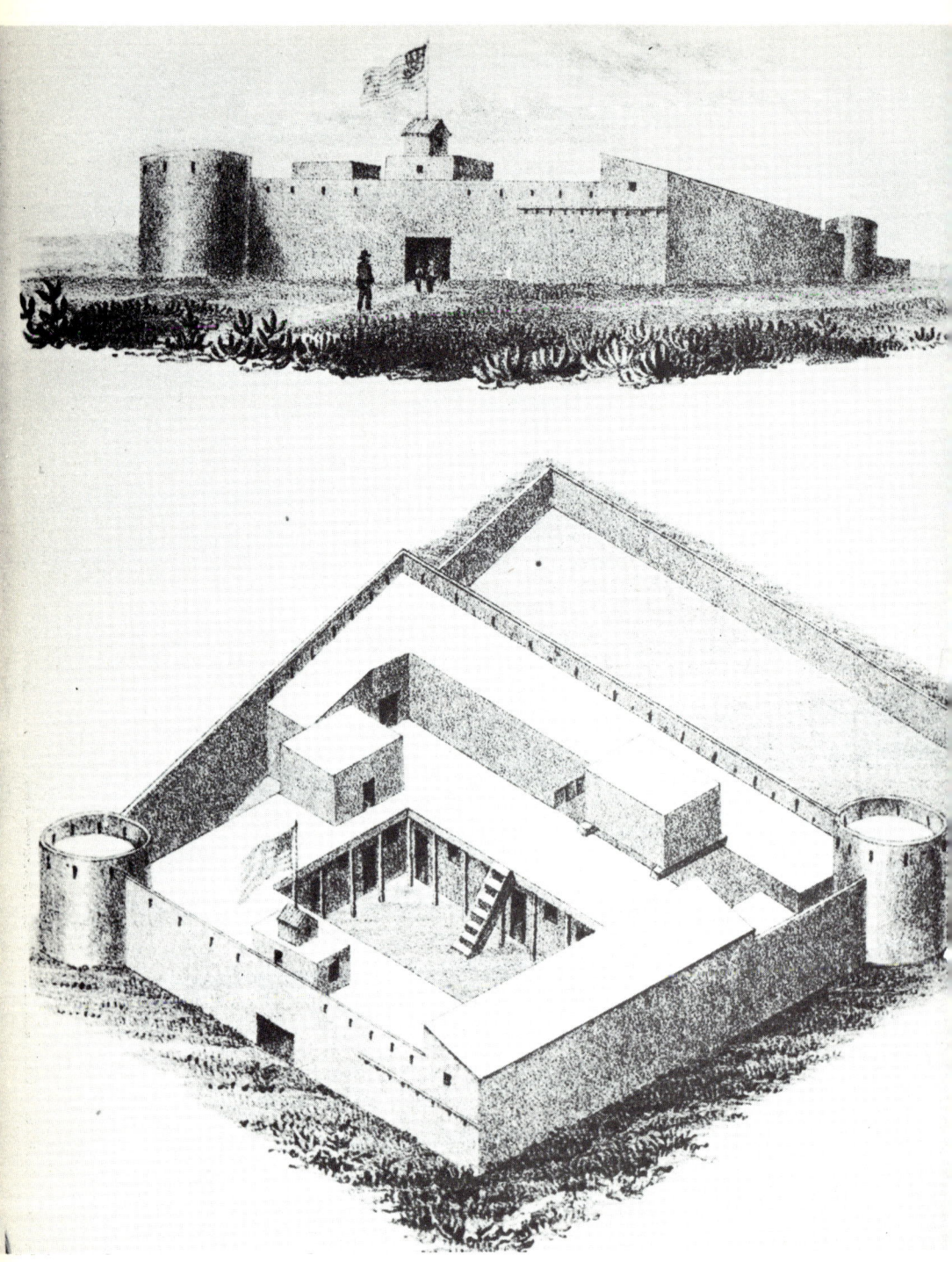

BENT'S FORT.   This is Bent's Fort in the early days of the Santa Fé Trail. Like the forts at Laramie and the Alamo, it was built round a courtyard. It also has watchtowers on the outside walls. At first it was a fur trading post but soon became a useful stop-over place for emigrants going to Santa Fé. In the later part of the nineteenth century, Bent's Fort became quite civilized. It had kitchens, a billiard room, an icehouse for champagne and various other comforts for the trail-weary travellers.

THE CONESTOGA WAGON.   This is the kind of wagon used by emigrants to travel to the West. It is roughly 3m long and 1½m high. The wagons were ordinary farm vehicles which were adapted to the emigrants' needs. Canvas was arched over the top to keep everything dry and warm. There were some-times pockets lining the inside of the canvas to carry small things. A well-off family might be able to bring two or more wagons; there was very little room for sleeping when the wagon was full of all the food and equipment needed for the journey.

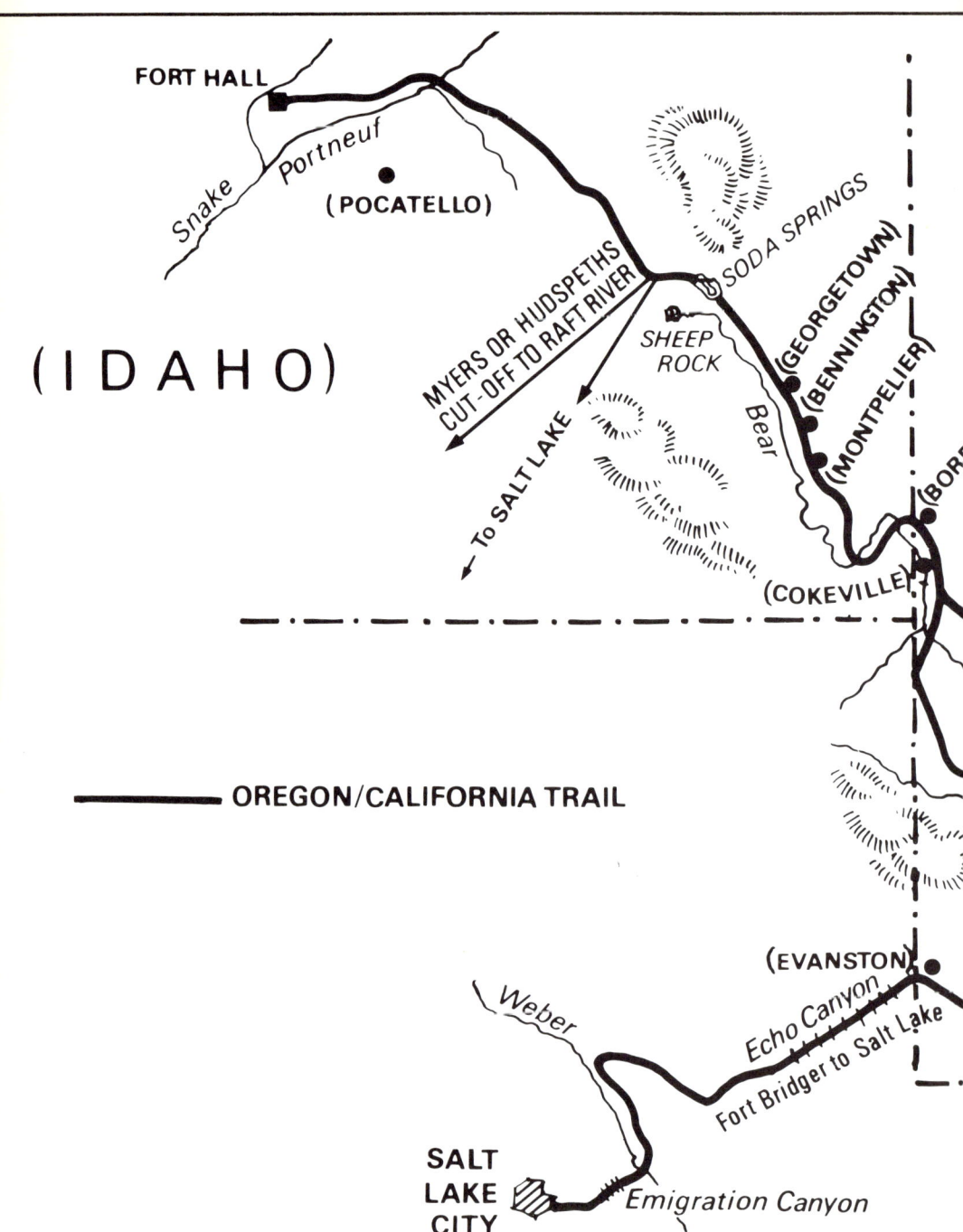

FORT HALL

Snake

Portneuf

(POCATELLO)

(IDAHO)

MYERS OR HUDSPETHS
CUT-OFF TO RAFT RIVER

To SALT LAKE

SHEEP
ROCK

SODA SPRINGS

(GEORGETOWN)

(BENNINGTON)

(MONTPELIER)

Bear

(BOR

(COKEVILLE)

——— OREGON/CALIFORNIA TRAIL

(EVANSTON)

Weber

Echo Canyon

Fort Bridger to Salt Lake

SALT
LAKE
CITY

Emigration Canyon

34

(WYOMING)

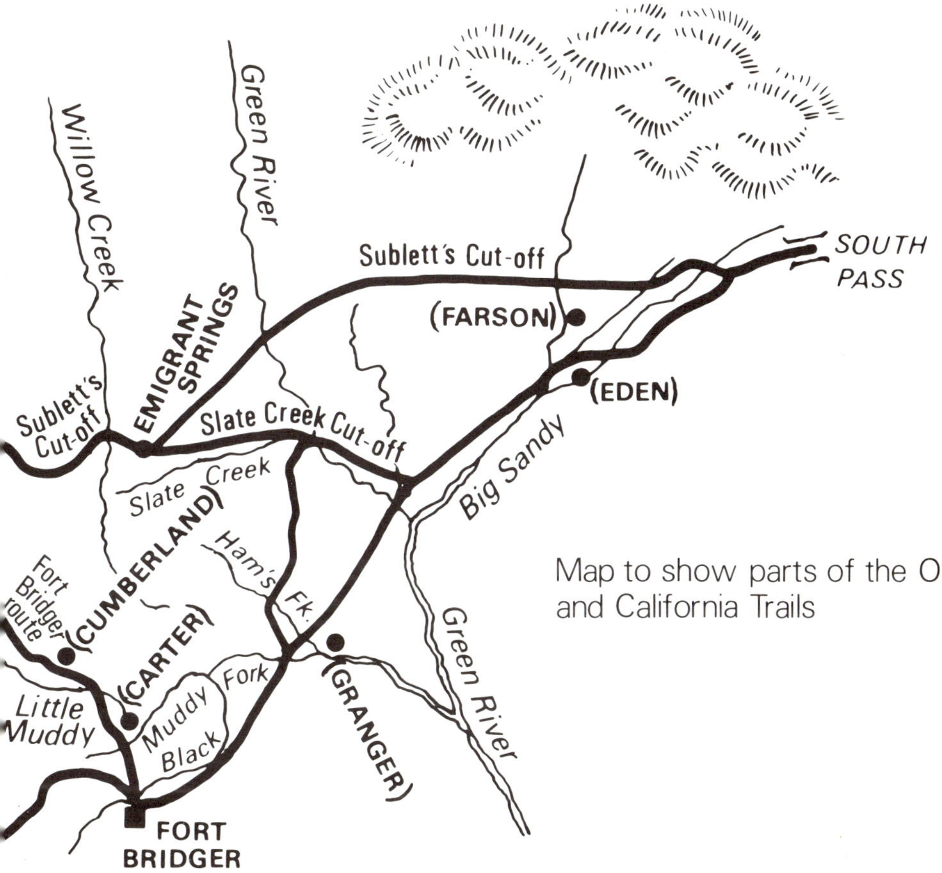

Willow Creek

Green River

Sublett's Cut-off

SOUTH PASS

(FARSON)

EMIGRANT SPRINGS

Sublett's Cut-off

Slate Creek Cut-off

(EDEN)

Big Sandy

Slate Creek

(CUMBERLAND)

Ham's Fk.

Fort Bridger route

(CARTER)

Green River

Muddy Fork

Black

(GRANGER)

Little Muddy

FORT BRIDGER

Map to show parts of the Oregon and California Trails

0   15   60

kilometres

THE OREGON TRAIL.   The first wagon train was led
by John Bidwell and took the Oregon route to the
West in 1841. Before this time pioneers had made the
journey on horseback, but soon wagon trains became
the accepted way for the settlers to travel. Here is a
typical party of emigrants on the road. Some of the
men are riding or walking, while the women ride
inside the covered wagons, which are drawn by oxen.
Sheep have been brought along for food.

LIGHTNING EXPRESS. The emigrants had a long way to go and moved at a walking pace. The two men in the picture have even brought along a handcart. A start was made at daybreak, and the guides went ahead to find the best places to cross streams and the safest camping sites. There might be a train of fifty or so wagons stretching out for long distances. Progress was slow so that the animals did not get tired too quickly. There was always a halt at noon. No wonder this party has named its wagon the "Lightning Express".

AN EMIGRANT CAMP. These emigrants have drawn up to camp for the night. They look very happy and are about to cook the evening meal. In fact the journey would have been much more unpleasant. People often became ill, water supplies ran out and food was scarce. There was little wood to be found on the plains, and fires for cooking had to be made from buffalo dung. Children found the journey boring. Sometimes they got accidentally left behind, or were even run over by the wagon-wheels.

CROSSING A STREAM. Covered wagons could cross shallow rivers, although a dangerous current might overturn them. There was always a danger that the wagon-wheels might get stuck in the mud. The animals were often tired and had no strength left to pull the wagons. You can see how the horseman in the picture is trying to urge the oxen across. Everything a family owned was inside the wagon and it was a disaster if the vehicle or animals were lost.

COMANCHE ATTACK. Comanche Indians terrorized people on the Santa Fé Trail. They lived in the barren, treeless plains of the south-west, and were very savage and warlike. You can see from the picture how open to attack the emigrant parties were on the Great Plains. The Comanche circled round the camp before they attacked, leaning to the side of their horses to avoid the bullets.

PIONEERS DEFENDING A WAGON TRAIN. At night the emigrants placed their wagons in a circle so that they would get some protection if the Indians attacked. The group in the picture are putting up a good fight. The animals have been brought in behind the wagons, and three men with guns are trying to shoot down some of the Indian leaders. In the early days the Indians fought with bows and arrows, or lances and tomahawks. They could shoot up to eight arrows in the time it took to reload the old-fashioned rifles used by the emigrants.

THE DONNER PARTY. This is Donner Lake, high up in the Sierra Nevada Mountains, where over half the Donner Party died on the California Trail in 1846. The emigrants reached the lake during a very bad winter. Trapped by the snow in impossible conditions, they could not keep their wagons warm although they covered the canvas with buffalo skins. They were unable to get out to chop firewood, and their last oxen and horses wandered away during the storms. When rescue parties finally reached them in the spring they found that the survivors had kept alive by eating the dead bodies of their comrades.

DONNER PARTY IN THE SIERRA NEVADA. Here some members of the Donner party are struggling across the Sierra Nevada Mountains to get help for their friends by the lake. The man in the foreground has made some snowshoes out of oxbows and hides. Eight of the nineteen who had set out died, but all five women in the party were among the survivors. No wonder California seemed like heaven to emigrants who had crossed over the Sierras in conditions like these.

RED RIVER OX-CARTS. Minnesota became an American territory in 1849, and in 1851 the Sioux Indians handed over large areas of their lands to the government. The settlers in these new lands started a trade in furs with the Red River settlers in Canada. Every year a procession of ox-carts carrying pelts arrived at St Paul, a Mississippi port. You can see the long line of carts approaching, watched by the Indians. The skins are being loaded onto a Mississippi steamboat to be taken down the river for sale in the fur markets.

THE MORMONS. The Mormons took the westward trail for religious reasons. The founder of the church was Joseph Smith. His *Book of Mormon* was published in 1830. Smith and his followers made a number of converts and sent missionaries as far away as Britain. Here is a picture of Smith preaching to a group which includes some Indians. Other settlers were against the Mormons and drove them away from the new towns where they tried to settle. The final blow was when Joseph Smith and his brother were charged with causing a riot and hanged in 1844. This convinced the Mormons that they should move to the free lands of the West.

BRIGHAM YOUNG. Brigham Young took over from Joseph Smith as head of the Mormon church. He looks like an ordinary Victorian gentleman in this picture. In fact he was an unusual and powerful leader. In 1846 he led the Mormons westward to Salt Lake in Utah, where he decided they should build a new city. The Mormon religion allowed a man to have more than one wife. This was because there were more female converts than men, and children were needed to colonize the area. When Young died in 1877 he left seventeen wives and fifty-six children.

MORMON HANDCART EMIGRANTS. Other Mormon groups followed the first pioneers. In 1856 some migrants attempted the journey with handcarts. You can see how difficult it must have been for the pioneers to drag their carts through rough country. The carts were about 1m long, and would only carry about 8kg. It was cheaper to go this way, but it must have been very hard, especially in bad weather. Ten parties of Mormons got to Salt Lake like this between 1856 and 1860.

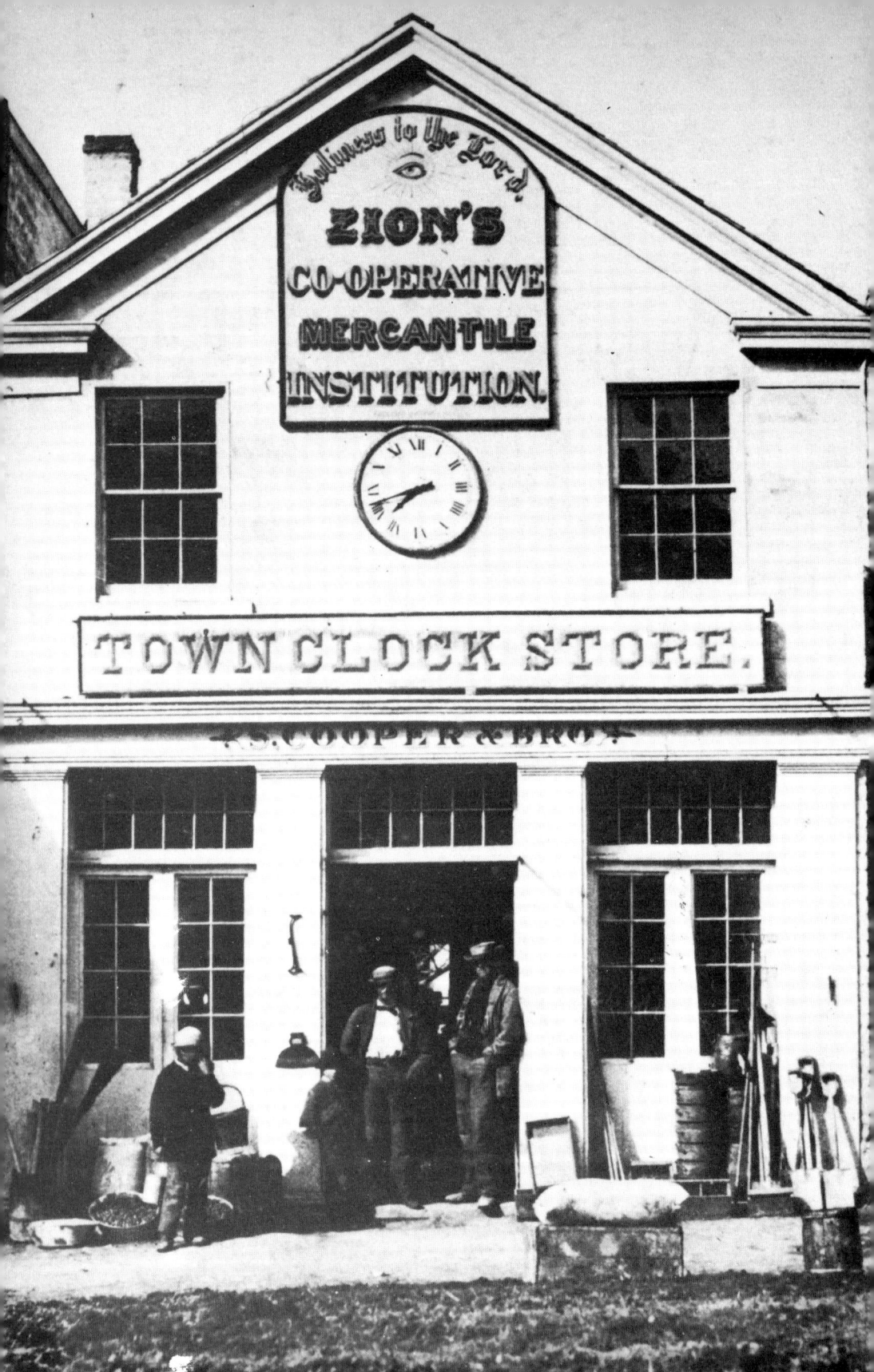

SALT LAKE CITY. The early years in Salt Lake Valley were hard. Clothes, wood, furniture and tools were all in short supply. Everything had to be brought across the desert. But the Mormons were very hard-working and gradually Salt Lake City took shape. This is a very early photograph, taken in 1857, of a town store. The church played a part in all Mormon activities. As you can see from the notice, this is a co-operative store under church guidance.

THE PIONEERS. Pioneers continued to make their way to the West throughout the nineteenth century. Farmers, doctors, lawyers and tradesmen came along, and helped to set up the new towns. These are two typical emigrant families who have had their photographs taken during a halt on the trail. They would have had to live like gypsies for many months. When they arrived at their destination they had to build their own house and farm the land.

3. The Gold Rush

On 24th January, 1848, gold was discovered at this sawmill in California, which belonged to John Sutter. It was found by one of the workers in the river below the millwheel on the left of the picture. The word quickly got round and by 1849 emigrants poured into California. So many people were attracted by the prospect of a quick fortune, that the mass emigration was known as the "Gold Rush". The prospectors were called the forty-niners after 1849, the year of the Rush. Some emigrants came by the difficult land route that had led to the Donner Party tragedy a few years earlier; others arrived by sea. People came from Europe and Britain as well as from other parts of America. Fortunes were made overnight and often gambled away the next day. Not everyone was lucky and found gold, although in the early days there were stories of large nuggets found by chance in streams and crevasses in the mountains. Fortunes were also made by the traders who followed the forty-niners to the West, and sold them the equipment and food they needed. San Francisco quickly became a booming town. The boom lasted well into the 1850s and caused whole new areas of the West to be opened up for settlers.

CALIFORNIAN MINING COUNTRY. You can see how beautiful the quiet Californian countryside looked when the forty-niners first arrived. Before the Gold Rush only a handful of Spanish-American ranchers lived there. Mining soon changed all this. Here are some miners looking for gold in one of the streams running down from the Sierra Nevada Mountains. Some little log houses are in the distance which the miners have built as temporary homes.

52

A ROUGH ROAD TO THE MINES. In the picture Below, a party of forty-niners is crossing a rough road in the Sierra Nevada Mountains on the way to the gold fields. Travellers had to be sure to cross the mountain range before the snows came during the autumn. In their hurry to stake a claim to the best gold mines, forty-niners often left their goods and wagons on the way. Mexican horses usually drew the wagons as they were used to the harsh, stony country. The men in the picture have tied ropes to their wagon to stop it turning over on a steep bend in the path.

BY SEA TO CALIFORNIA. These men are making the journey to California by sailing ship. It was often easier for someone living in Boston or New York to go this way, although the 20,000 km sea trip round Cape Horn took much longer than the land route. You can imagine how boring it must have been for the men to sit on deck like this, day after day, for at least six months. Conditions were cramped and the food was bad. One passenger complained that the pork was rusty, the dried beef rotten and "there were two bugs for every bean". To make matters worse there were fierce storms and rough seas in the Cape Horn area.

THE FORTY-NINERS. This group of forty-niners is arriving in California by the overland route. After the Sierra Nevada, the green fields and lush vegetation of the country must have been a wonderful sight. The men are carrying shovels and pickaxes, and have a donkey to carry some of their cooking equipment and bedding. A small bullock-drawn cart follows. The forty-niners used to buy their clothes and equipment before they set out, as it was always expensive to buy things at the gold fields.

A PROSPECTOR. This is how a prospector looked after he had been working the mines for some time. He wears a tattered woollen shirt and heavy trousers. This man's shoes have worn thin, but miners usually wore boots. His wide-brimmed hat gives protection from the Californian sun. Two pistols are at his belt, and his pack includes a pickaxe, shovel, panning equipment and a drinking mug. His hair and whiskers are uncut and probably unwashed as well.

PANNING FOR GOLD. The most common way of taking gold from the streams was by panning. The man in this picture is using a metal pan. This is first filled with earth and gravel from the river bed. It is then filled with water. By swirling the contents around any gold is separated from other materials. The miner would have to stand in cold water all day. Prospectors usually worked in pairs with one doing the digging and the other the panning. The pan could of course also be used in the evening for cooking, and carrying drinking water.

THE CRADLE. Miners also used the cradle method to get their gold. The idea behind this was similar to the pan washing method. The device looked like a child's cradle on rockers. You can see the two men on the right filling their cradle with gravel. The cradle was about 1m long and would take much more earth than a pan. It needed two men to do the digging, another to fill the cradle and a fourth to pour in the water. A cradle could cost as much as a hundred dollars if bought at the gold fields.

THE SLUICE. These two men are using a simple sluice to wash out the gold. A sluice had iron bars inside. These were known as riffle boxes and were able to catch the gold as water poured over the gravel. These two men have found a quiet spot on the river. Soon it was found that the old methods were much too slow and big companies with complicated machinery took over.

A LONG TOM. These men are posing proudly for their photograph in front of a "Long Tom" sluice. As you can see, the gravel was piled into the box at the end of the water-shoot. The gold particles, which were heavier than gravel, were caught on bars in the riffle box underneath. The man in the middle is holding a gold pan. Perhaps there are some nuggets inside it.

GAMBLING.   Miners played cards all the time at the camps. On Saturday evenings gambling schools were set up where poker or faro were played for money. These places later became the Wild West saloons you can see in Hollywood films. This picture shows some nasty-looking characters playing faro. The man on the left of the table looks like a Mexican. The two men in city clothes are card-sharpers who have come to swindle the miners out of their gold.

A MINING TOWN IN 1860. Once the miners married, or brought their familes out West, the first settlements became more permanent. Streets were laid out, and schools, hotels and other large buildings sprang up. Town life started to develop. Newspapers were founded and the stage coaches began to call at regular intervals. This is a picture of Cisco Station. It is changing from a mining camp into a small town. Permanent wooden buildings have been put up and there is a lot of traffic in the streets. A group of Indians are camping beside the road on the left.

WELLS, FARGO & CO. Banks grew up in the new mining towns to deal with the miners' gold. This advertisement for the Wells, Fargo Bank dates from 1856. The company's stage coaches carried the gold in strong boxes under the driver's seat. Passengers also went along, so the small isolated new mining towns were gradually joined up with the rest of America. Bandits sometimes attacked the coaches to steal the gold.

PIKE'S PEAK. Towards the end of the 1850s the original gold mines were becoming worked out. The gold seekers next turned towards Pike's Peak in Colorado, where there had always been stories that gold could be found. The emigrants wrote on their wagons, "Pike's Peak or bust" on the outward journey. Those returning sometimes put "Busted, by God" as not everyone was successful. However the gold rush brought settlers to Colorado, where some stayed to set up homes and farms.

COMSTOCK SILVER MINES. Another wave of emigrants went to Nevada, where gold and silver deposits were found about the same time as the Colorado boom. Silver mining needed new methods as the metal was embedded in quartz rocks. Shafts were dug all over the countryside. This picture was made at the Comstock mines during the 1870s. By that time mining was in the hands of large companies. These miners work an eight-hour shift underground and receive regular wages.

73

74

4. Life on the Frontier

The mining boom ended during the 1850s and 60s, and large companies took over the strikes. The last wave of settlers in the West came to the plains and grasslands in the 70s and 80s, after railways had opened up the area. Slowly western America became more civilised. Roads and regular transport joined up the communities of the first settlers. Professional people arrived in the new towns, and there were now women and children in the mining areas. In 1860 large parts of the country were still in Indian hands, but by 1890 the tribes had been almost wiped out.

Cattle had always been raised on the frontier. The coming of the railroad meant that western ranchers could bring their cattle to the east for sale. In 1867 Joseph G McCoy persuaded Texan ranchers to drive their animals north to Abilene. Here the herds would be put on board the Kansas Pacific railway to be sold in the eastern states. Cattle ranching produced the West's most well-known character, the cowboy. This man is trail boss, and responsible for leading herds of cattle across the prairies. His broad-brimmed, Stetson hat will shelter him from the sun. The back of his neck is protected by a scarf which can also be put over his mouth if he runs into a dust storm. Fringed leather chaps (leggings) over his trousers protect his legs from spiky branches, and he is wearing high-heeled leather boots. His gauntlet gloves are made from the best buckskin. He has a gun at his belt, and binoculars in his hand.

THE ROUND-UP. Cattle were rounded up twice a year, in spring and in autumn and taken to market. Each animal was caught with a lasso, like this one. As the cattle lived on the open prairie for most of the year, a rancher had to know exactly which animals were his. He did this by branding the cattle with a special mark to show the ranch they came from. New calves were branded at the round-up.

THE LONG DRIVE. Here are some fine looking long-horn cattle being driven north to Kansas or Nebraska. Often several ranches grouped together to make up a herd of 2,000 to 3,000 head of cattle. The trails started in spring after the round-up, and covered about 15 to 25km in a day. The party was headed by the trail boss, and other cowboys rode at the side to stop the animals straying. Sometimes the cattle became frightened, and stampeded. This could be very dangerous, and the cowboys had to gallop ahead, firing their guns, and try to turn the leaders round.

A BUCKING BRONCO. This cowboy is trying to break in a wild mustang to the saddle. Even today Texan cowboys sometimes demonstrate the skill of riding "bucking broncos" at rodeos. The artist who drew the picture was Frederic Remington. He journeyed in the West in the 1880s, and produced hundreds of drawings of life on a cattle ranch for American papers.

THE WELLS FARGO STAGE. Supplies were brought to the first settlers in freight wagons drawn by oxen. In 1858 the first horsedrawn stage coaches appeared. They carried mail, as well as passengers and valuables. After the Civil War of 1861-5 every large town in the West had a Wells Fargo stage coach office. Here you can see a typical coach crossing the San Marcos Pass in California. Nine people could be squeezed inside the coach, and twelve sat on top. The vehicle was called a "Concord". It had special leather straps fixed to the underside so that it swayed on rough roads, instead of bumping passengers up and down.

MAIL COACH ATTACK   This is a familiar scene to those of you who watch western films. Indians and bandits often attacked the stage coaches. Armed guards, like those shown in the picture, had to be hired to go with the coach, particularly when gold was being carried. There was an incident like this one in the autumn of 1854, when Sioux Indians ambushed the Salt Lake City stage. They killed three men and took $10,000 worth of gold bullion.

PONY EXPRESS. Another way of carrying mail was by Pony Express. A man on horseback could go faster than a stage coach. The first express delivery service was started between St Joseph, Missouri and San Francisco in April 1860. The ride took ten days, compared with twenty-two days by stage coach. It was much too long for one man, so riders and horses were changed at regular intervals.

THE TELEGRAPH SERVICE. By October 1861 the Pony Express had been replaced by the telegraph. In the picture the Pony Express rider is waving to the men who are fixing the telegraph wires. The Indians were mystified by the pylons stretching out over the countryside. They called the telegraph line the "singing wire" or the "whispering wire" because of the noise it made when a message was being transmitted.

HOMESTEADERS. The Homestead Act of 1862 brought families into West Kansas and Nebraska. It allowed settlers to take over 160 acres of land for a fee of ten dollars. All they had to do was to live there and farm the land. After five years the farm would belong to them. This family's house is built from lumps of turf. As you can see, the building has no windows, and is very small. These houses were not very pleasant to live in. They were damp and cold, and the water dripped through in wet weather.

INDIANS ATTACK A HOMESTEAD. The settlers moving into the West often took the territory from the native Indians. In the early nineteenth century, the US Government had made treaties with the tribes. These treaties guaranteed protection for the Indians' homelands. But they were often ignored by the settlers. The Indians fought back. Here a party is raiding an isolated homestead. The men are putting up a brave fight, but the Indians have guns and are already inside the door. Frontier life in the West fascinated other Americans. Fiction writers like Mark Twain and Bret Harte wrote many stories about incidents of this kind.

82

BUILDING THE RAILROAD. The railroads had a great effect on the colonization of the West. The building of the railroad was done by veterans of the Civil War, and by workers who had come from Ireland. A good deal of the heavy work was done by Chinese people. A group of them are standing on the right of the picture cheering the first locomotive on the Central Pacific Railroad.

LINKING THE RAILROADS. The Central Pacific Railroad went east from Sacramento, while the Union Pacific started at Omaha and went west. The two lines met, with great ceremony, on May 10th, 1869 at Promontory, Utah. This photograph was taken on the historic occasion. You can see that the two trains are not quite the same. The Central Pacific locomotive on the left burned wood, while the Pacific engine on the right used coal. It also has a smaller funnel. The two railroad presidents are shaking hands in the middle of the crowd. After the official opening of the completed line, which linked America from coast to coast, there were a good many parties and celebrations.

INDIANS DESTROYING RAILROAD TRACKS. Indian tribes feared and hated railroads over their land. They attacked the construction workers and in 1867 the Cheyenne wrecked a Union Pacific freight train and massacred its crew. You can see the desolate flat country of the plains which the railroad crossed. The Cheyenne are attacking the line with picks and shovels and burning the sleepers.

VIGILANTES. Parts of the West remained wild and lawless throughout the nineteenth century. Mining towns in Montana drew a very vicious crowd of bandits, and volunteer groups called "vigilantes" were formed to help keep the peace. The vigilantes were ordinary citizens but their justice was rough. This group have just hanged their sheriff, Henry Plummer. He had been running the Plummer Gang of stage coach robbers.

RED CLOUD. This is a photograph of the powerful Sioux chief, Red Cloud. He was the only Indian chief to win a war against the United States. He wished to prevent white men using the Boxeman Trail across Sioux territory. After peace talks had failed, Red Cloud led the Sioux in a series of attacks against soldiers, who were building forts along the route. The Indians massacred Captain Fetterman and eighty men. In 1868 Red Cloud won his point, and US troops were ordered out of the area. Later Red Cloud visited Washington and New York, and won sympathy for Indian rights.

CHIEF SITTING BULL. This is another famous Indian leader, Chief Sitting Bull of the Hunkpapa Sioux. He fought at the battle of the Little Big Horn in which General Custer died in 1875. He was a wise and respected leader and lived in Standing Rock Reservation for many years. He even took part in Buffalo Bill's Wild West Show. Tragically, he was killed for resisting arrest in 1890.

GERONIMO. The Apaches were another fierce Indian tribe who harassed people in the south-west. Their last and most famous leader was Geronimo. He is on the right of this group with three of his Apache warriors. He surrendered to General Crook in 1886 and was sent into exile. By this time the Apache were wearing a strange mixture of Indian and European clothes, and were armed with rifles. They had an unfortunate liking for European alcohol which made them even more fierce and unpredictable.

THE WESTERN FILM. The great pioneering days of the West are remembered in fiction and films. By the end of the nineteenth century artists and writers from the eastern states and from Europe were journeying in the West, and trying to picture the old days. Fiction writers were fond of stories about battles with Indians, of fortunes made in the Gold Rush and the life in the frontier towns. There were many songs about the cowboy's lonely life. In the twentieth century the cinema took over. Many westerns give a very good idea of the beautiful countryside of the West. But they do give an over-romantic view of life there. This film still is from *Red River*, with Joanne Dru and John Wayne.

Table of Dates

1803	The Louisiana Purchase took place.
1804	Lewis and Clark expedition set out.
1820s	The Santa Fé Trail opened.
1822	The Rocky Mountain Fur Company founded.
1830	*The Book of Mormon* published.
1835	The battle of the Alamo fought. Texas was taken from Mexico.
1841	The first emigrants took the Oregon Trail.
1843	The "Great Emigration" took place. (200 families took the Oregon Trail.)
1844	Joseph Smith was hanged.
1845	Texas became a state.
1846	The Mormons founded Salt Lake City. The Donner party set out on the California Trail.
1848	Gold found at Sutter's Mill.
1850	California became a state.
1858	First regular stage coaches began running.
1859	Oregon became a state.
1860-1	The Pony Express was in operation.
1861-5	American Civil War was fought.
1861	Kansas became a state.
1862	Homestead Act was passed.
1864	Nevada became a state.
1867	Nebraska became a state.
1869	Union Pacific and Central Pacific railroads met.
1876	Colorado became a state.
1886	Geronimo surrendered.
1889-90	Dakota, Wyoming, Montana, Idaho and Washington became states.
1890	The Battle of Wounded Knee was fought.
1896	Utah became a state.
1907	Oklahoma became a state.
1912	Arizona and New Mexico became states.

New Words

Backwoodsman	A man who lived in the uncultivated part of the country.
Barter	Trading by exchange of goods and not by money.
Brave	A Red Indian warrior.
Card-sharpers	People who cheat at cards to make money.
Cowboy	A man in charge of cattle on a ranch.
Emigrant	A person who moves to settle in a different country or state.
Faro	A gambling card game where bets are placed on the order of appearance of cards.
Frontiersman	A man who lived on the frontier or the border between settled and unsettled country.
Homestead	An area of land granted to settlers to build their homes on.
Lasso	A long rope with a running loop at one end, used for catching wild horses or cattle.
Mormons	A religious group also known as the "Latter Day Saints".
Nugget	A rough lump of untreated gold.
Panning	A method of finding gold by washing gold-bearing gravel.
Poker	A gambling card game where bets are placed on the value of a hand.
Prospector	A person who looks for gold or other metals.
Railroad	Railway.

Rancher	A person who runs a place where cattle are bred.
Stockade	An enclosure or fortification made with upright, wooden stakes.
Strike	A find, for example of gold or oil.
Telegraph	An apparatus or system for sending messages to distant places by means of wires and electricity.
Trail	A path or route.

More Books

American Heritage, *History of the Great West* (1965).

Barbara Currie, *Pioneers in the American West 1740-1840* (Longman 1969)

Lucius Beebe and Charles Clegg, *The American West* (Bonanza Books, New York 1965).

Robert J Hoare, *When the West was Wild* (A & C Black 1976).

Frank Humphris, *The Story of the Cowboy* (Ladybird 1972).

Frank Humphris, *The Story of the Indians of the Western Plain* (Ladybird 1973).

Robin May, *The Wild West* (Look-in. Independent Television Books 1975).

Jack Schaefer, *Shane* (André Deutsch 1954).

Time-Life Books, *The Old West — The Forty-niners* (1974).

Time-Life Books, *The Trail Blazers* (1973).

Index

Picture Credits

The author and publishers wish to thank the following for the pictures which appear in this book:

Pat Hodgson 25, 27; Radio Times Hulton Picture Library 6, 10, 11, 12, 17, 18, 45, 48, 52-3, 54, 55, 58, 59, 60, 62, 63, 64, 65, 66, 67, 68-9, 71, 72-3; United Artists 92; The Wayland Picture Library 28, 36, 46, 49; The Western Americana Picture Library *Frontispiece*, 8, 9, 13, 14-15, 16, 19, 20, 21, 22, 23, 24, 26, 30, 31, 32, 33, 37, 38, 39, 40, 41, 42, 43, 44, 47, 50, 56, 57, 61, 70, 74, 76, 77, 78, 79, 80, 81, 82, 83, 84-5, 86, 87, 88, 89, 90, 91.